Mauro Magni

To Manage Windows With a USB Pen Drive

Portable Programs

Using applications on a pen drive can sometimes be handy for testing new programs without creating anything on the hard disk and operating system registry.
Sometimes these programs can help us to repair a crashed computer.

Second Edition: Jun 2012

© Mauro Magni - lulu.com

Cover: Mauro Magni photocomposition
(The cover image shows the distribution of files on the hard disk of a computer)

ISBN-13: 978-1477580127
ISBN-10: 1477580123

Table of contents

INTRODUCTION 4

WHAT PROGRAMS ARE PORTABLE? 5

SECURITY AND ANTIVIRUS 6
    ClamWin portable 6
    Dr.Web CureIt..10
    Spybot - Search & Destroy Portable 13
    Eraser..17

HARDWARE AND SOFTWARE INSTALLED..21
    System Information for Windows..21

UTILITY FOR THE OPERATING SYSTEM...24
    WinDirStat..24
    CCleaner...27
    Smart Defrag 33
    Toucan...38
    Recuva 40
    System Explorer...44

UILITIES...48
    Advanced Console 48
    7-Zip..50

HOW TO CREATE OUR SUITE OF PORTABLE SOFTWARE...54

SUITE PORTABLE READY TO USE 58

HOW TO CREATE A PORTABLE PROGRAM 62

CONCLUSION 64

Introduction

The "portable programs" are programs that do not require installation on our computer and you can run directly from pen drive (USB flash drive) and, in general, leave no trace on the computer on which they were executed. The portable programs are no different from those installed, in fact, are exactly the applications that we all know, reconfigured (sometimes re-written by programmers in ad hoc versions), so they do not require the creation of files among folders user and neither the addition of keys in the registry of the computer that executes them.

Often versions "portable" are distributed in an official way by their own developers, other times they are created by third parties who convert existing open source programs and adapt them for use directly from USB memory flash drive.

Why use these programs? They may be useful to people who work, move frequently and don't have the opportunity to take with them their computers. Or, a collection of portable programs can be particularly helpful to those who need some software to use in emergency conditions, for example to fix a crashed computer. We can simply use them to run tests new programs without "dirtying" the hard drive and the operating system's registry.

What programs are portable?

The no-install programs, portable or standalone are software which does not require installation, does not "dirty" your hard drive and Windows registry. Most of them are GNU, GPL (free software) or freeware, are multilingual, can be used by everyone and are installed on a USB stick, for use on another computer, keeping our settings.

Do not install a program on your computer means that there is neither in the registry keys or system files, no reference to the presence of these programs and then work independently on the system without leaving a trace.

To better understand the meaning of what it means "do not install" a program, let's run from the Internet to download the Firefox browser portable. Then copy the files into any folder on your hard drive and then launch the browser. Surfing the Internet, browse history, cookies, temporary files are stored within the folder where we copied the files of Firefox portable. This means that it is the only folder that contains all references to the use of the Firefox browser. If instead of the hard drive we used a pen drive (USB key), all of our surfing activities would remain with the browser only and only on the pen drive; in the hard disk, there would be no trace of the use of Firefox portable. I can now remove USB key from my computer and, after placing it in another, the Firefox portable browser "remembers" all configurations made earlier.

So we can summarize that a program is defined as portable if:

- Should not be installed on the guest computer to run
- No problems if you run it from any guest computer's support, internal or external
- Do not leave traces in Windows registry, nor in the user folder, nor in any other directory on the guest computer, but only in the folder from where you ran it
- It must not modify the configurations of equivalent programs that are already installed on the guest computer

Security and Antivirus

ClamWin portable

ClamWin Portable is a free Open Source GPL (GNU GPL provides the user freedom to use, to copy, to edit and the programs deployment) with which to scan the operating system. You can install it on a pen drive; (USB key), Ipod, on a portable hard disk, or CD / DVD and use it on any computer, without leaving a trace of personal information. It can be installed on the following operating systems: Windows 2000/XP/Vista/7. You can download it from the following site
http://portableapps.com/apps/security/clamwin_portable.

Figure 1

By pressing the red button "**Download**", you will see the following screen:

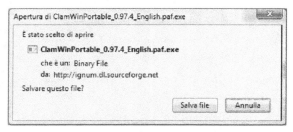

Figure 2

After pressing the **"Save File"** button, on our USB pen drive will have the file
ClamWinPortable_0.97.4_English.paf.exe.
Double click with the mouse on the file above and you will see the screen from which to begin the installation.

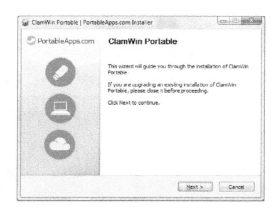

Figure 3

Press the "**Next>**" key and you will see the following screen:

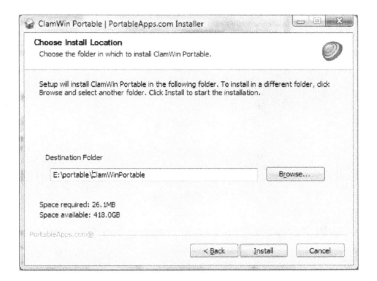

Figure 4

In the "**Destination folder**" enter the name of the directory to install the product and then press the "**Install**" button; you will see the following screen:

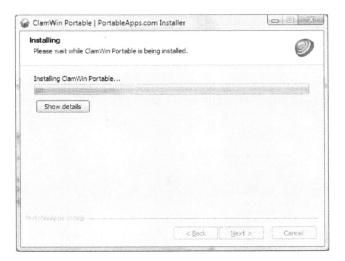

Figure 5

At the end of the installation, you will see the following screen:

Figure 6

After selecting "**Run ClamWin Portable**", and after pressing the "**Finish**" button will display the following screen:

Figure 7

After pressing the "**Yes**" button, we will see the following screen where the program searches the manufacturer's website and install the latest program updates:

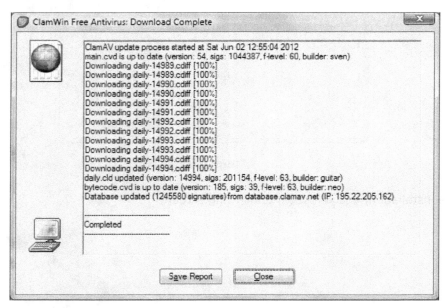

Figure 8

Press the "**Close**" key and you will see the main product screen (Figure. 9) in which you can select, for example, the units (**C**) to be checked and next press the "**Scan**" button:

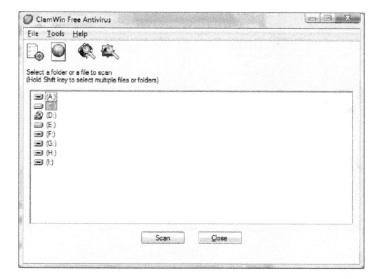

Figure 9

During the scan operation will appear some screen like this one:

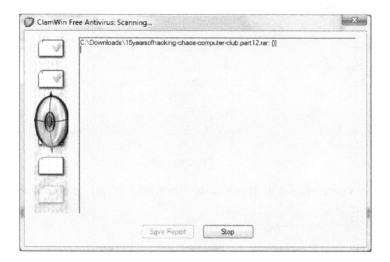

Figure 10

At the end of scan we will see the screen like this one:

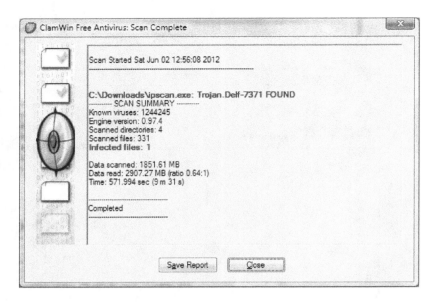

Figure 11

By default, ClamWin only displays a report, when it finds the virus.as shown in Figure 11.
We can change the default from the "**Tools**" and then the "**Preferences**" of the main screen (Figure 9) in which we have to choose between two options: "remove" or "move to quarantine folder". The advice is to set the option "move to quarantine folder" so that the virus is neutralized and we can analyze the situation calmly. It can happen, in fact, that some files are reported as viruses that actually are not.
In the directory where you installed ClamWin, you can see three directories, an executable and a help file:

Nome	Ultima modifica	Tipo	Dimensione
App	02/06/2012 12.54	Cartella di file	
Data	01/06/2012 9.36	Cartella di file	
Other	02/06/2012 12.54	Cartella di file	
ClamWinPortable.exe	10/04/2012 7.22	Applicazione	135 KB
help.html	08/04/2012 23.15	Firefox Document	6 KB

Figure 12

During the run, ClamWin **reads (and writes) only** from and in the directory in your USB pen, where you installed it.

Dr.Web CureIt

Dr.Web CureIt is a free antivirus and antispyware that "cure" an infected computer. It can detect and remove the most common threats such as worms, email viruses, viruses, key loggers, dialers, adware, hack tools, backdoors, Trojans and more.
It can be installed on the following operating systems: Windows 2000/XP/Vista/7.
You can download it from the following site:
http://www.pendriveapps.com/drweb-cureit-stand-alone-antivirus-utility/

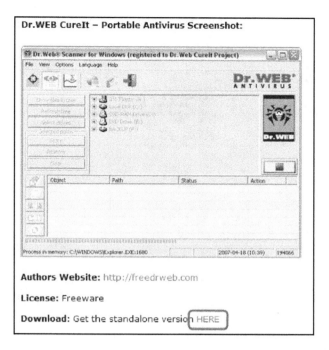

Figure 13

Place your mouse over the word "**HERE**" (in the blue box) and click; the following screen will appear:

Figure 14

Press the "**Save File**" and the download will be activated automatically, at the end, in your USB pen drive will be transferred the program **cureit.exe**.
To launch it, double click on the program and you will see a screen where you must first press the "**OK**" key and another screen, where you have two choices "**Start**" and "**Update**".
Press the "**Update**" button to update the antivirus to the latest changes, once the process is finished, press the "**Start**" button. During this phase, for safety reasons, the computer executes only and only the **cureit.exe** program while all the other programs (including those potentially infected) are locked (Figure.15).

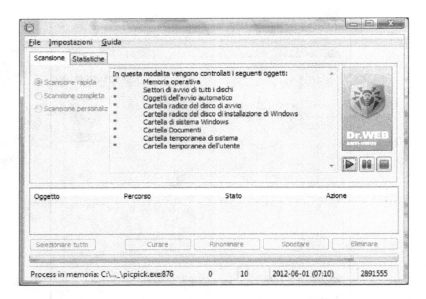

Figure 15

When an object infected, with a known virus is detected, Dr.Web Scanner, automatically, attempts to cure it as shown in the Figure.16.

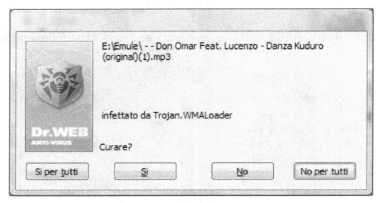

Figure 16

In this case if our answer is "**Si per tutti**" / "**Yes to all**", then every time Dr.Web finds a virus, will attempt to "cure" automatically.If curing fails, the infected object will be moved to the quarantine. Suspicious files are displayed in the special report field in the bottom side of the main window.

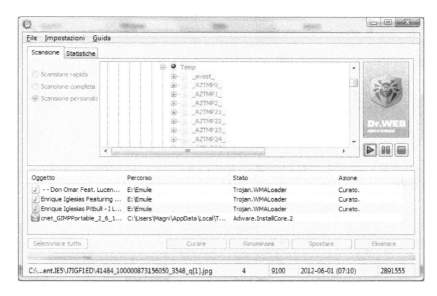

Figure 17

After scanning, Dr.Web will present a screen (like to the above) which will list any viruses or malware found on your computer. Dr.Web will try to cure objects infected with a known virus, don't perform any operation for suspected files. For these, there are four buttons: Cure, Rename, Move and Delete which we will use once analyzed suspected files.

It's necessary to clarify that the use of this program, is absolutely free for home computer but not for other purposes so if you use it in a company, you must purchase a license.

Spybot - Search & Destroy Portable

Spybot - Search & Destroy detects and removes thousands of spyware and malware. It is able to "clean" the hard drive files no longer required (and beyond) and solve the Windows registry problems. Spybot is freeware for personal use. Many cleaning and immunization require the administrator account. It can be installed on the following operating systems: Windows 2000/XP/Vista/7.

You can download it from the following site:

http://portableapps.com/apps/security/spybot_portable

Figure 18

We proceed, then, to download the **SpybotPortable_1.6.2_Rev_2.paf.exe** file and at the installation as described in Figures 2, 3, 4, and 5: the procedure is always the same.

After installation, the content of the directory is the following:

Nome	Ultima modifica	Tipo	Dimensione
App	01/06/2012 12.35	Cartella di file	
Data	01/06/2012 13.28	Cartella di file	
Other	01/06/2012 12.35	Cartella di file	
help.html	26/10/2010 1.31	Firefox Document	6 KB
SpybotPortable.exe	04/01/2011 7.27	Applicazione	132 KB

Figure 19

To launch the application, select the **SpybotPortable.exe** file and after double click of the mouse, you will see the following screen:

Figure 20

After pressing the "**Next**" button (located in the lower left corner of figure.20), will see the screen shown in the figure.21, where will press the "**Search for updates**" button to download the latest product updates and after we will press the "**Next**" button:

Figure 21

Now we will see the screen shown in figure.22, where we will press the "**Immunize this system**" button and later, after you have protected the system, we will press the "**Next**" button.

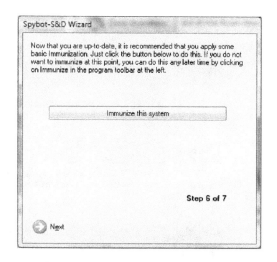

Figure 22

At this point the last screen will be shown, where pressing the "**Start using the program**" (Figure.23) will launch the application (set of programs) and the program's main screen will appear (Figure.24).
The procedure described will be executed only the first time we use the product, and later, after when you will click twice on the **SpybotPortable.exe** program, the initial screen will be shown (Figure 24):

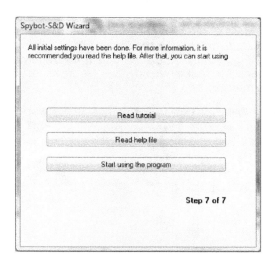

Figure 23

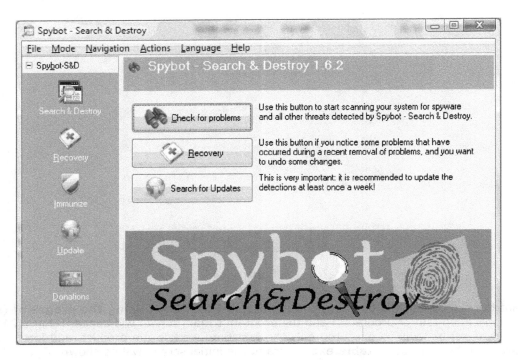

Figure 24

To start the scan, press the topmost button on the right side of the screen "**Check for problems**" and a screen like that of Figure 25 will be displayed. In the lower left corner, we read the type of check carried out at this moment (enlargement of Figure 26). The scanning time depends on the number of files on disk (or disks) analyzed. It is a good idea to make weekly the updates of the product by pressing the button "**Search for Updates**" from the main screen (Figure.24).

Figure 25

Running bot-check (1871/1296572: NSIS Media Extension)

Figure 26

Spybot is a freeware program (software distributed with or without source code). The use of the program is bound to a license that allows free redistribution. The freeware software in use is granted without fee, and is freely distributable and duplicable.

Eraser

Eraser is an advanced security tool for Windows that allows you to completely remove sensitive data from your hard disk by overwriting the data multiple times. We think that when we delete data from a hard drive, it no longer exists.
Unfortunately, it does not. When you delete a file, the operating system does not really remove it from the disk, but deletes only the reference from the file systems table. The file remains on disk until another file is created over it, so until this moment, it may still yet be recovered. That's why we use programs like **Eraser** which instead provides for the complete removal of the deleted file, but that is still present on disk. **Eraser** is a Free / Open Source (GPL), so we can use without purchasing a license. It can be installed on the following operating systems: Windows 2000/XP/Vista/7.
You can download it from the following site: ***http://portableapps.com/apps/utilities/eraser_portable***

Figure 27

We proceed, then, to download the **EraserPortable_5.8.8_English.paf.exe** file and at the installation as described in Figures 2, 3, 4, and 5: the procedure is always the same.
To launch the application, select the **EraserPortable.exe** file and after double click of the mouse, you will see the following screen:

Figure 28

There are two ways to erase data: **On-Demand** or **Scheduler**.

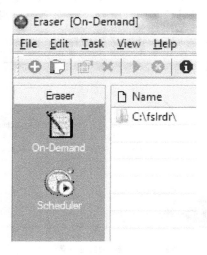

Figure 29

On-Demand means that the file is removed immediately, and **Scheduler** means that we can set a frequency or time of execution (every day, only a few days of the week, etc.).
First, we select the way of execution of Eraser, choosing **On-Demand** or **Scheduler** option (Figure.29); next we press "**File**" and then "**New Task**" (Figure. 30)

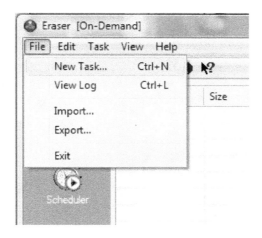

Figure 30

We select the unit "**Unused space on drive**" a shown in the figure 31 or the directory "**Files in folder**" as shown in figure 32 and then we press the **OK** button.

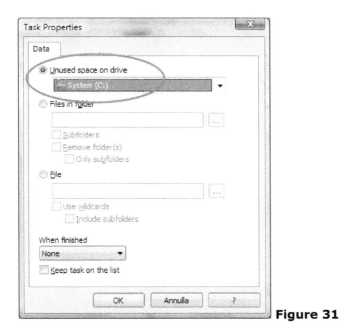

Figure 31

Figure 32

You will see a screen like to Figure 33 where, by selecting the unit (for example C) or the directory name (in our example C:\fslrdr\) and pressing the right mouse button will display a menu (Figure. 34) where, by selecting the "**Run**" option, will be start the deletion process.

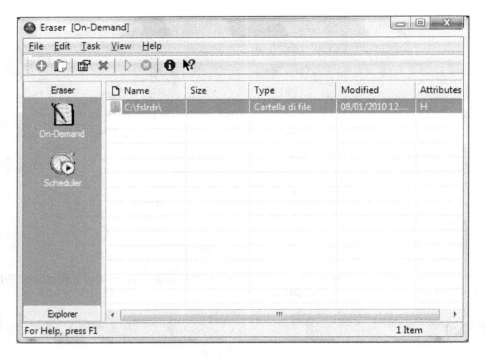

Figure 33

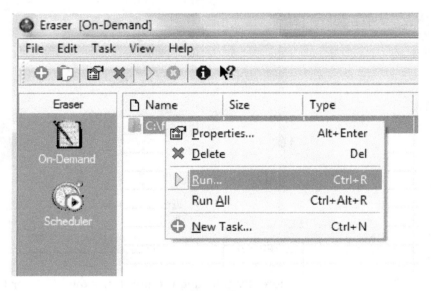

Figure 34

I note that the process of cancellation of **Eraser**, interest only, and only the files still exist on disks, which have already been canceled.

Hardware and software installed

System Information for Windows

SIW is a tool for Windows that scans your computer and collects detailed information on system properties and settings and displays them in an intuitive way. SIW can create reports in CSV, HTML, TXT or XML for PC Software and Hardware Inventory, Asset Inventory, software license management, Security Audit, Configuration Management Server. The product is distributed in the professional version for a fee, while the Home Edition can be freely used without a license but only for personal purposes (only on your home computer).

It can be installed on the following operating systems: Windows 2000/XP/Vista/7.

You can download it from the following site ***http://portableapps.com/apps/utilities/siw_portable***

Figure 35

We proceed, then, to download the **SIWPortable_2011.10.29.paf.exe** file and at the installation as described in Figures 2, 3, 4, and 5: the procedure is always the same.

To launch the application, select the **SIWPortable.exe** file and after double click of the mouse, you will see the following screen:

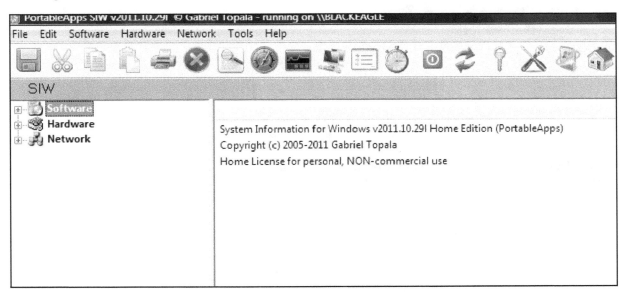

Figure 36

The screen is divided into two sides; the left, in which there are three categories **Software**, **Hardware** and **Network** and the right side in which there are the details of the individual resources as shown in Figure.36 and Figure 37.

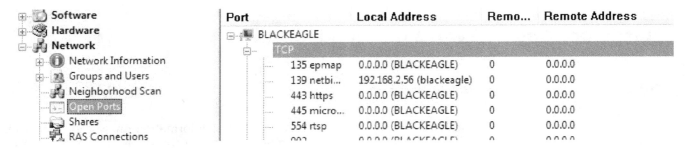

Figure 37

SIW is a very complete tool that displays every detail, hardware and software, of our computer. In particular, there is a section that allows you to view all the passwords you have saved on your computer; select the "**Passwords**" from the menu on the left and a screen like of Figure.38 will be displayed, where (in this case) were found two password (obscured for security reasons).

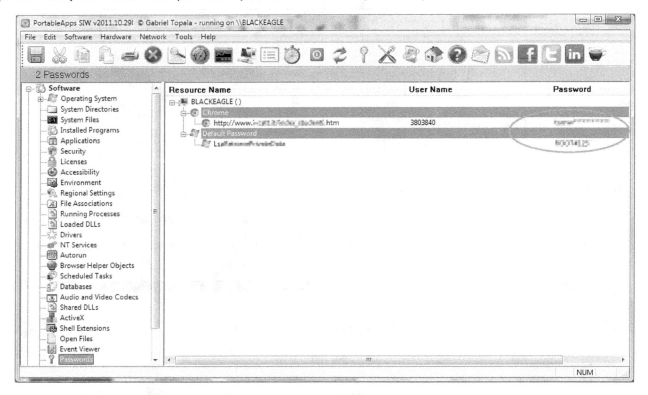

Figure 38

Or, again from the left menu, selecting the "**Licenses**" option will see a screen like the following that lists all licenses, for all products installed on our computer.

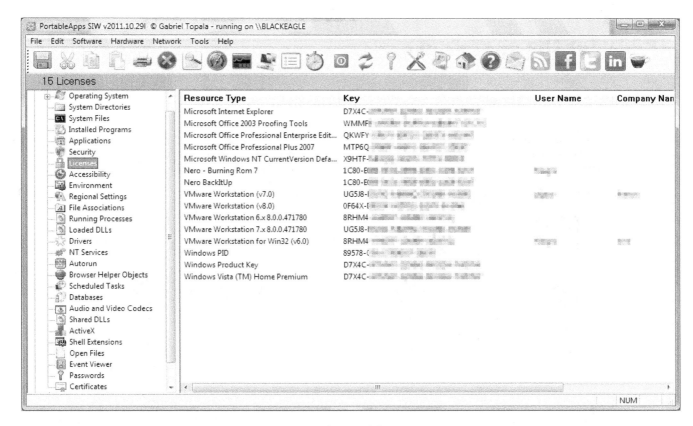

Figure 39

Utility for the operating system

WinDirStat

WinDirStat is a program, open source GPL, for Windows, very handy for its graphical interface, which analyzes the use of a disk (or disks) of the operating system, for a subsequent "cleaning" option.
It can be installed on the following operating systems: Windows 2000/XP/Vista/7.
You can download it from the following site
http://portableapps.com/apps/utilities/windirstat_portable#

Figure 40

We proceed, then, to download the **WinDirStatPortable_1.1.2.80.paf.exe** file and at the installation as described in Figures 2, 3, 4, and 5: the procedure is always the same.
After the installation, from the directory where we have performed the installation, select the **WinDirStatPortable.exe** file and after double click of the mouse, will see a screen like this one (Figure.40), where you can see a small yellow icons in motion that indicate the operation of the program during the analysis phase of the operating system disks:

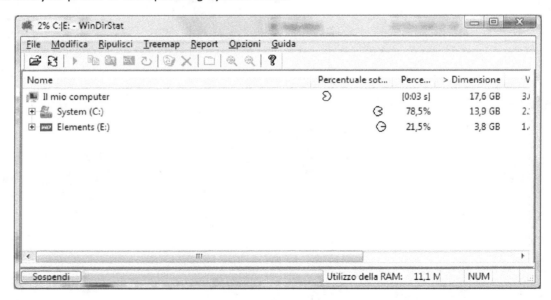

Figure 41

The duration of the analysis depends on the number of disks installed in the system and the number of files on each disk. The program analyzes each file and determines its occupation on the disk. At the end of this phase, will see a screen like the following:

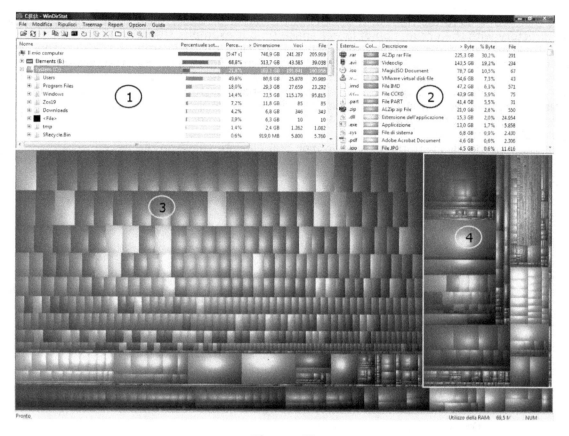

Figure 42

We can divide the screen into 4 zones, indicated by the numbers 1, 2, 3 and 4.
The zone number 1 lists the names of disk drives and shows the space occupied by files on the drive as shown in figure 43:

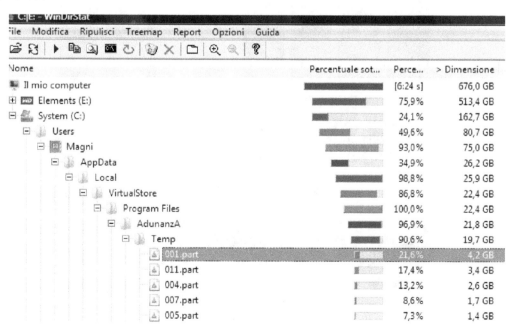

Figure 43

If we want to know what are the files or directory that takes up more space, we click the mouse at the unit that interests us (for example, C or E) and appears the list of directories with their occupation of space on

25

the drive (colored lines to the right of the name of the file or directory). We scroll down the screen until we find the directory with the occupation of larger space (in our example, **Users** on **C** drive of figure 43). If now we want to know which file occupies more space, we click on the name of the directory and browsing through directories and subdirectories in the tree as shown in figure 43, you will find the file being searched. In our sample, the file's name is **001.part** (21,6 %) in the subdirectory **Temp**. The zone number 2 (Figure.44) lists in descending order the occupation of space on the drive, depending on the file extension. From this perspective we can know the types of files that take up more disk space. Selecting an extension with the mouse, for example **.rar** (Figure.44), simultaneously in zone 3 will be displayed areas with the same color of extension **.rar**, white bordered (Figure.45).
They represent all the files with the extension **.rar** that allocate space on the drive.

Estensi…	Col…	Descrizione	> Byte	% Byte	File
.rar		ALZip rar File	225,3 GB	33,3%	199
.avi		VLC media file (.avi)	143,5 GB	21,2%	234
.iso		MagicISO Document	72,7 GB	10,8%	63
.v…		VMware virtual disk file	54,6 GB	8,1%	43
.cc…		File CCKD	43,9 GB	6,5%	75
.part		File PART	41,4 GB	6,1%	31
.dll		Estensione dell'applicazione	15,2 GB	2,2%	24.587
.zip		ALZip zip File	13,9 GB	2,1%	508
.exe		Applicazione	12,7 GB	1,9%	5.639
.sys		File di sistema	6,8 GB	1,0%	2.414
.jpg		File JPG	4,4 GB	0,7%	10.515
.pdf		Adobe Acrobat Document	3,8 GB	0,6%	2.080
.img		ALZip IMG File	3,1 GB	0,5%	6
.doc		Microsoft Word Document	2,7 GB	0,4%	1.250

Figure 44

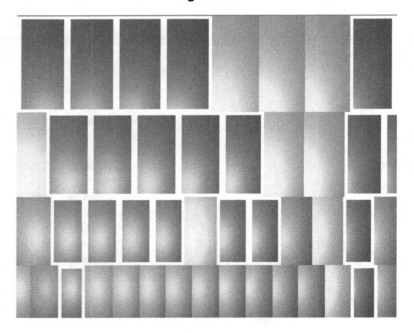

Figure 45

Zones 3 and 4 of Figure.42 represent all files, respectively, allocated on the disk drives E and C. If in the zone number 1 we select the C drive, simultaneously a white margin around the zone 4 will appear, as shown in the figure.46. Therefore, if we select the E drive, simultaneously a white margin around the zone 3 will appear.

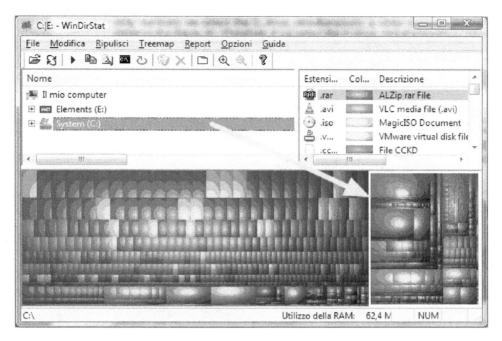

Figure 46

In zone 4 (Figure.46) selecting a rectangle with the mouse (indicated by a white box), simultaneously in zone 1,we will see the name of the corresponding file, while in the left bottom of the screen will be displayed ,the directory and the file name selected.

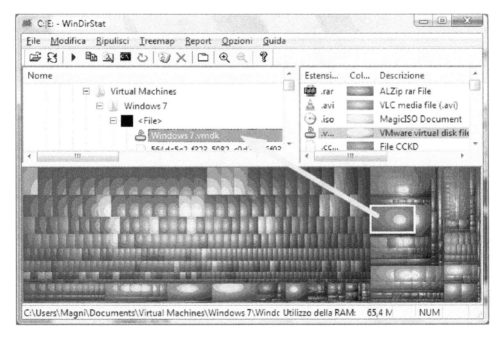

Figure 47

This utility is very interesting because it allows us to immediately identify which directories and files takes up more space on our disks.

CCleaner

CCleaner is a tool to keep your computer "clean". Protect your privacy online and make your computer faster and safer. It removes temporary files, the history, cookies from the following browsers: Internet Explorer, Firefox, Google Chrome, Opera, and Safari. It Cleans the Recycle Bin, Recent Documents, Temporary files and logs of Windows. It Removes voices, old and no longer used, from the Windows registry. On the manufacturer site there are versions "free" and paid. We will download the free and portable version from the following site:
http://www.piriform.com/ccleaner/download/portable. Now we press the "**Start Download**" key and unpack the zip file **ccsetup319.zip** into a directory of the USB pen drive.

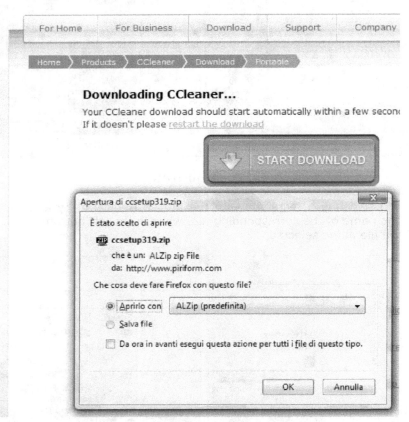

Figure 48

In the directory, double click on the **CCleaner.exe** file and will see the following screen:

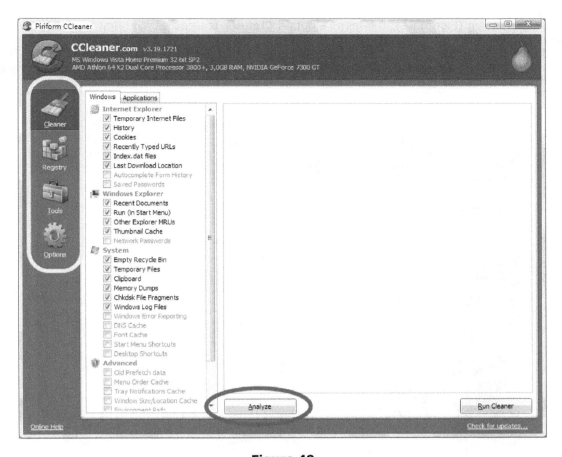

Figure 49

On the left side of the screen of figure 49, there are four menu items: **Cleaner, Registry, Tools, and Options** (highlighted in yellow). In the next menu (on the right side of the screen), under the tab of Windows (Figure.50), there are kinds of objects that will be analyzed:

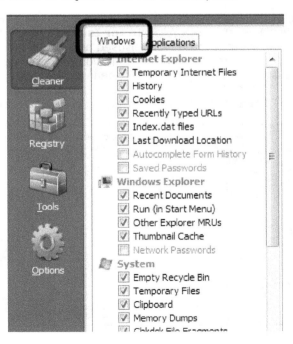

Figure 50

When CCleaner is run (Figure.51), the menu's option **Cleaner** is selected (the first top left); to proceed with the analysis, press the button "**Analyze**" on the lower left of the screen and at the end of operation, will be displayed on the right side of the screen all the exceptions that are to be removed (Figure.51). To proceed with removing the files, press the button at the bottom right "**Run Cleaner**" and then confirm by pressing "**OK**" on the next screen:

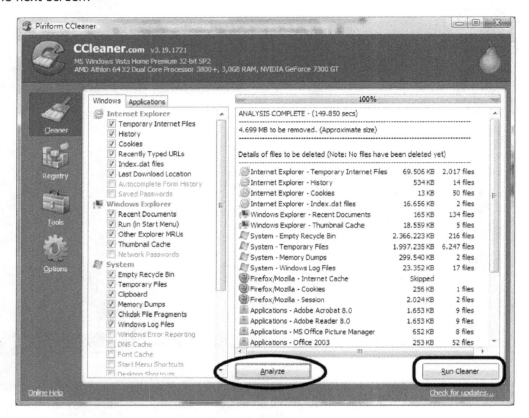

Figure 51

To proceed with the cleaning of the registry entries from the main menu of Figure.49, select "**Registry**" (the second top left) and will be displayed the button "**Scan for Issues**", at the bottom left. After pressing it, CCleaner will analyze the log entries that are no longer used and in the right side of the screen will display the list of those to be deleted. Once complete, on the right side of the screen will found the button "**Fix Selected Issues**". When pressed, another screen will appear asking if you want to back up the log entries before proceeding. Answering "**Yes**" will be given a new screen that will ask the path and name of the backup file; after pressing the "**Save**" button, the following screen will be shown:

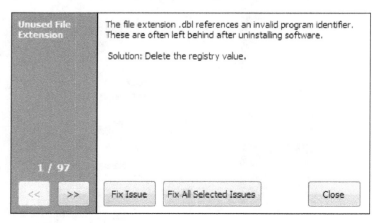

Figure 52

Instead, answering "**No**", the screen in Figure 52 will be immediately displayed.

30

Pressing the "**Fix All Selected Issues**" button, the selected registry entries will be removed.
By selecting "**Tools**", the third menu item of the Figure.49, the following screen will be displayed:

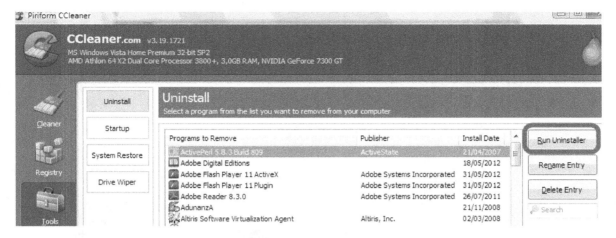

Figure 53

There are four menu items: **Uninstall, Startup, System Restore, Driver Wiper**. Pressing the "**Uninstall**" button, selecting the program to remove and pressing the "**Run Uninstaller**" button, we are able to uninstall all programs that are listed in the middle of the screen.
Pressing the "**Startup**" button, will see the following screen:

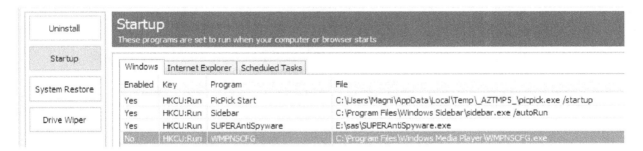

Figure 54

We see three tabs: **Windows, Internet Explorer, and Scheduled Tasks**, each of which contains the list of programs that run automatically when Windows and Internet Explorer starts. To disable the automatic startup of these programs, select the entry by mouse and double-click on first column on the left, the value (in column) changes from "**Yes**" to "**No**" and vice versa.

Yes	HKCU:Run	Sidebar	C:\Program Files\Windows Sidebar\sidebar.exe /autoRun
Yes	HKCU:Run	SUPERAntiSpyware	E:\sas\SUPERAntiSpyware.exe
No	HKCU:Run	WMPNSCFG	C:\Program Files\Windows Media Player\WMPNSCFG.exe
No	HKLM:Run	Adobe ARM	"C:\Program Files\Common Files\Adobe\ARM\1.0\AdobeARM.exe"
No	HKLM:Run	Adobe Reader Speed Launcher	"C:\Program Files\Adobe\Reader 3.0\Reader\Reader_sl.exe"

Figure 55

By selecting "**System Restore**" (figure.53) instead, the system administrator is able to remove restore points of Windows operating system as shown in the following screen:

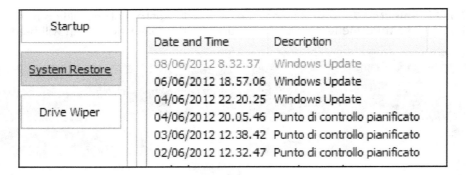

Figure 56

When we delete a file, Windows removes the reference to this one, but don't physically delete it from the disk. This means that, with appropriate software, someone could reconstruct everything or parts of deleted files. For privacy and security reason, you can set CCleaner to clean the areas free from the drives (hard drives and removable) of the operating system so that deleted files can not be recovered. Selecting "**Wiper Driver**" from figure.53 will be shown a screen like figure 57. On the right side, select "**Free Space Only**", **Simple Overwrite(1 pass)**, the drive where you want to perform the removal and clicking the "**Wipe**" button, the files removed from the system will be overwritten and not to be more recoverable.

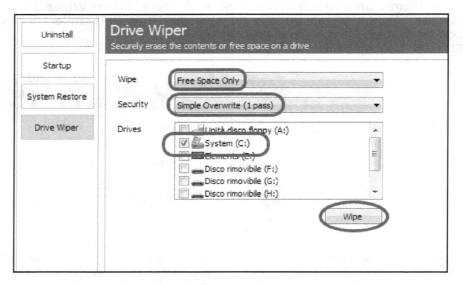

Figure 57

Carefully, to select the option in the Wipe field.

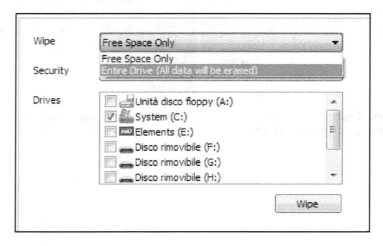

Figure 58

Selecting "**Entire Drive (All data will be erased)**", means that CCleaner program will erase all files on the disk. **WARNING**, this means that all drive's files will be erased.

Smart Defrag

With the continuous use of the computer (install and uninstall programs, creating and deleting files and folders), folders and files are fragmented. A file is fragmented, when it is stored in several places in the hard disk. The opening (reading) of a fragmented file is slow, because the operating system, before reading it, must reassemble the various pieces (fragments) that are located in different parts of the hard drive.

Smart Defrag is a disk defragmenter (streamlines disk space unused) powerful and fast with an easy interface to use. It's freeware for personal and business use. Like all the defragmentation utilities, it requires administrator privileges to run.

It can be installed on the following operating systems: Windows 2000/XP/Vista/7.

You can download it from the following site:

http://portableapps.com/apps/utilities/smart_defrag_portable

Figure 59

We proceed, then, to download the **SmartDefragPortable_2.3.paf.exe** file and at the installation as described in Figures 2, 3, 4, and 5: the procedure is always the same.

After the installation, from the directory where we have performed the installation, select the **SmartDefragPortable.exe** file and after double click of the mouse, will see a screen like this one:

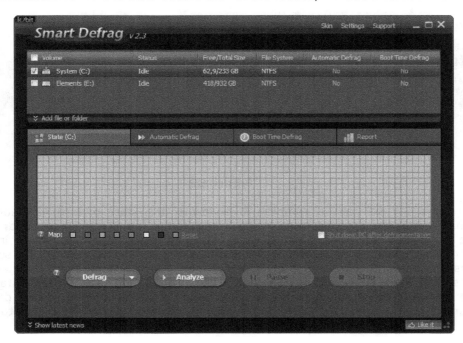

Figure 60

Selecting the unit of interest (in our case is C) and pressing the "**Analyze**" button, the program proceeds by analyzing the entire hard drive showing the different allocations of the files as displayed in Figure.61.

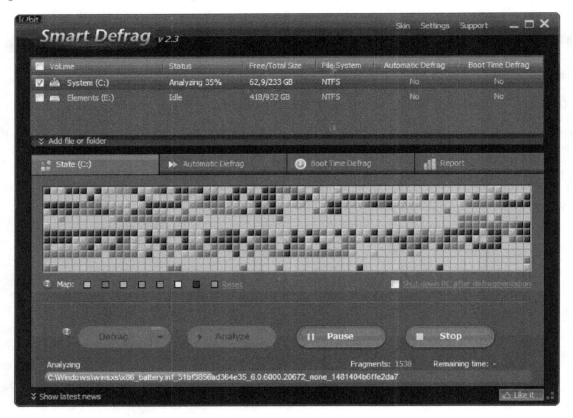

Figure 61

The meaning of colors in the little squares is obtained by placing the mouse over one of them; right of "**Map**" field; the penultimate small square shows the fragmented files (Figure.62)

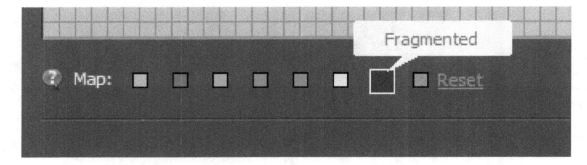

Figure 62

At first sight (Figure.61) we have a complete overview of the state of fragmentation of our disk. At completed scan, the program produces a report that indicated in the "**Recommendation**" box (left side of Figure.63) the suggested activities. In our case, "**Defrag and Fast Optimize**" indicates that the defragmentation would be recommended. In the **Summary** box, on the right of the screen there is the number of files scanned, the percentage of fragmentation and the number of fragmented files. At the bottom of the screen there is the list of fragmented files. To proceed with defragmentation, select "**Fast Optimize and Defrag**"; the duration of the process depends on the degree of disk defragmentation. If defragmentation is not necessary, you will find in the box **Recommendation**: "No need to defrag".

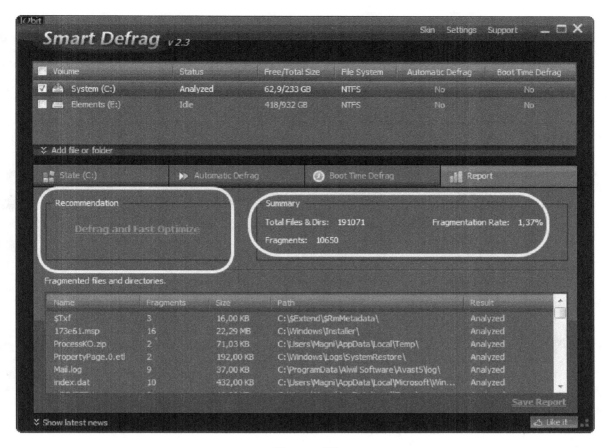

Figure 63

On the right of the screen (Figure.63), above, is located the "**Settings**" option, which after being selected will display the following screen:

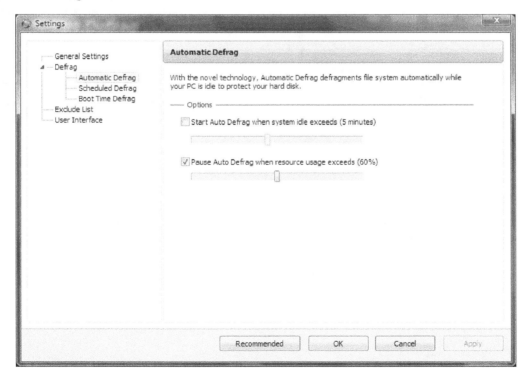

Figure 64

On the left side of the screen in Figure 64, select the menu item "**Defrag**" and below there are three options: **Automatic Defrag, Scheduled Defrag and Boot Time Defrag**. When we select the item "**Automatic Defrag**" (in a few moments we see how to activate it), the parameters on the right side of the screen indicate when to activate it (Start Auto Defrag When idle system exceeds (5 minutes)) and when restrict its operation (Pause usage ...... Exceed (60%)). By selecting the item "**Scheduled Defrag**" will be displayed a screen (Figure.65) where selecting "**ON**" on the right side of the screen, then selecting the unit (on which to run defrag) and pressing the "**Configure**" button, will be displayed the last screen (bottom of figure65), which allows us to specify how often to run the defrag.

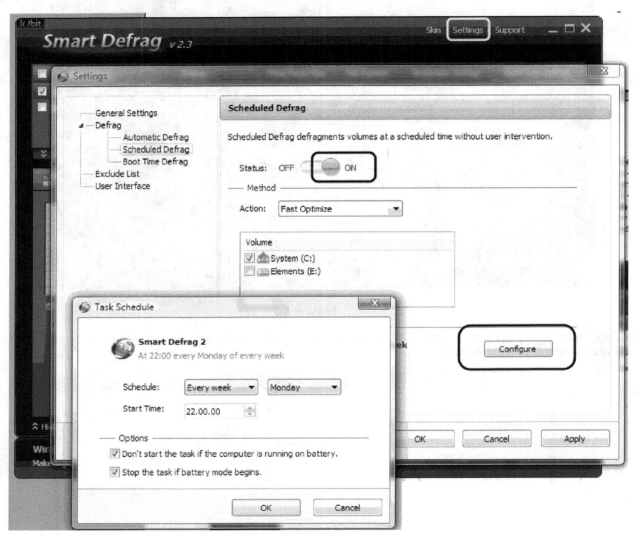

Figure 65

If we select the option "**Boot Time Defrag**" from the main menu (figure.64), the screen in Figure 66 will be displayed where we can specify when to run automatically the defrag after booting the computer.

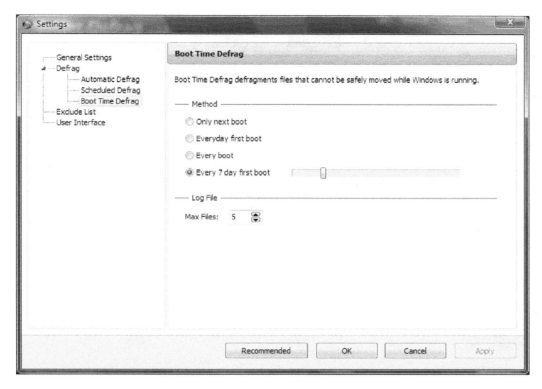

Figure 66

Toucan

Toucan is a utility that allows you to synchronize, backup and protect data securely, encrypting the data. We shall now only the back-up and refer the reader to the product site (the same as the download) for complete description of the other functions. Toucan backs up and data recovery (restore) in standard Zip, 7-zip and gzip files, with support for complete backups, updating existing backups and differential ones, and restore files from an archive.

It can be installed on the following operating systems: Windows 2000/XP/Vista/7.

You can download it from the following site: *http://portableapps.com/apps/utilities/toucan*

Figure 67

We proceed, then, to download the **Toucan_3.0.4.paf.exe** file and at the installation as described in Figures 2, 3, 4, and 5: the procedure is always the same.

After the installation, from the directory where we have performed the installation, select the **Toucan.exe** file and after double click of the mouse, will see a screen like this one:

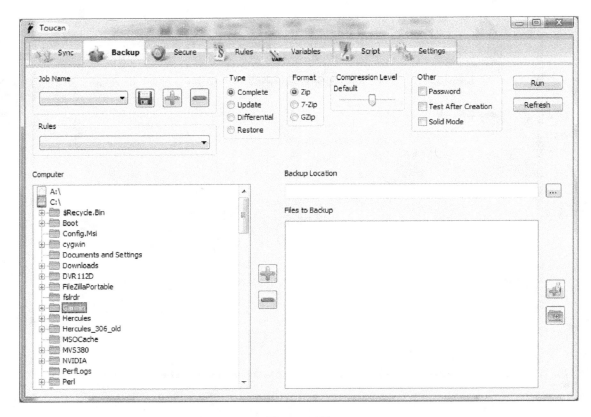

Figure 68

To back up the data, select the "**Backup**" tab in the upper left corner of the screen as shown below:

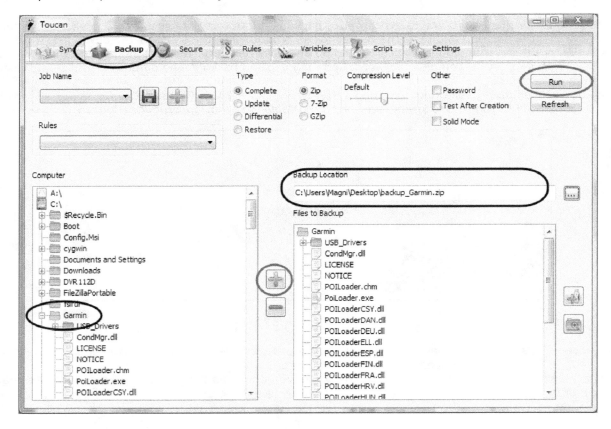

Figure 69

On the left side (Figure.69), select the directory to be saved (for us Garmin) and press the "✛" button in the middle of de screen, while the right side will display a list of files to be saved. Now we specify the path and filename to save the directory ("backup location") and press the "**Run**" button, to the right, at the top of the screen. When finished, you will see a screen like the following (Figure.70), which lists the file saved and the operation's result:

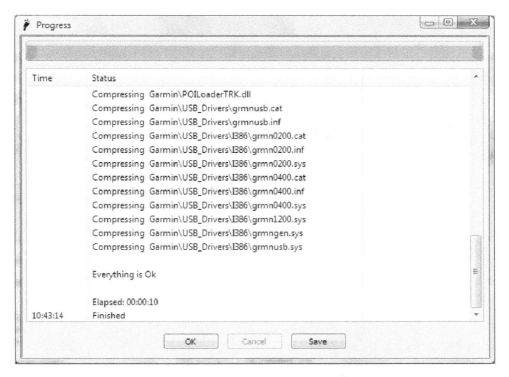

Figure 70

The backup file will be created in ZIP format, so, simply select it for restore and explode the files Zip contents to the desired directory.

Recuva

Recuva is a program that lets you recover any files that were accidentally deleted from your computer. It can also recover files from external devices such as removable hard drives, memory cards for cameras, MP3 players.
It can be installed on the following operating systems: Windows 2000/XP/Vista/7.
You can download it from the following site: *http://www.piriform.com/recuva/download/portable*
After pressing the "**Start download**" button, will see a screen that contains the file **rcsetup142.zip** (Figure.71): download and explode the contents of the zip file in the USB pen drive's directory. Inside we find two executable files: **recuva64.exe** and **recuva.exe**. To activate it, double click the mouse on one of the two files (the choice depends on whether the operating system is 32 or 64 bits).

Figure 71

After you start **Recuva**, a series of screens will appear:

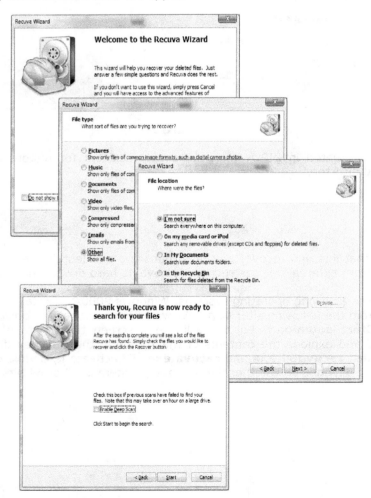

Figure 72

In the first screen of figure 72 "***Welcome to the Recuva wizard***", press the "**Next**" button, while in the second "***File Type***", select the last option "**Other**" (and then press **Next** button), in the following select the first option **'I' m not sure** "(and then press **Next** button) and in the last screen, press the" **Start** "button. You will see a screen like the following:

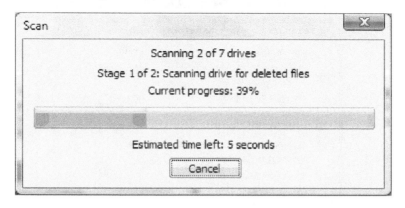

Figure 73

After running the scan of all drives in the computer, you will see the following screen:

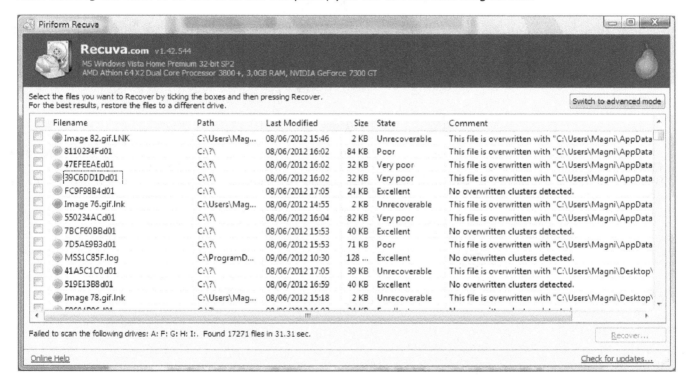

Figure 74

The first column "**Filename**" lists files names to retrieve, preceded by a coloured dot, the second screen contains the location of the file, the third screen displays the last modification date and the fourth screen, the file size. The penultimate column "**State**" displays the status of files that can be "*Excellent*", "*Poor*" or "*Very poor*" based on the fact that archives are "intact", "slightly overwritten" or "very overwritten". If the colored ball, next to the file name, is green, then the file is recoverable while if the colour is red, to know the probability of recovery, you read what is reported in the column "**Status**" as mentioned above. To retrieve the files, select them with the mouse, pressing the check box to the left of each file.

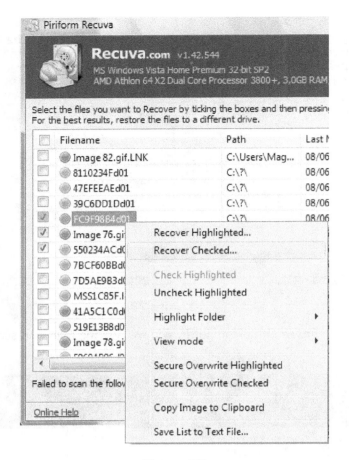

Figure 75

After selecting the files to be recovered, press the right mouse button and select the option "**Recover Checked**" in the next menu; you will then see another screen that will ask the location where to retrieve the file and after pressing the **OK** button, the files previously selected will be recovered, as shown in the next picture:

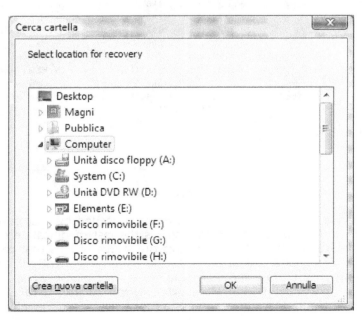

Figure 76

System Explorer

System Explorer is a task manager that automatically analyzes the processes of the operating system and produces detailed information about the activities, processes, modules of the system itself.
It can be installed on the following operating systems: Windows 2000/XP/Vista/7.
You can download it from the following site:
http://portableapps.com/apps/utilities/system_explorer_portable

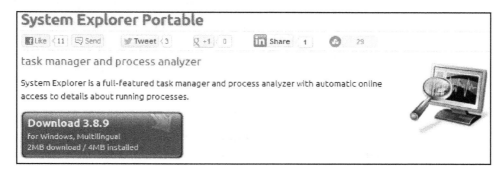

Figure 77

We proceed, then, to download the **SyatemExplorerPortable_3.8.9.paf.exe** file and at the installation as described in Figures 2, 3, 4, and 5: the procedure is always the same.
After the installation, from the directory where we have performed the installation, select the **SystemExplorerPortable.exe** (run it with administrator rights to have more features) file and after double click of the mouse, will see a screen like this one:

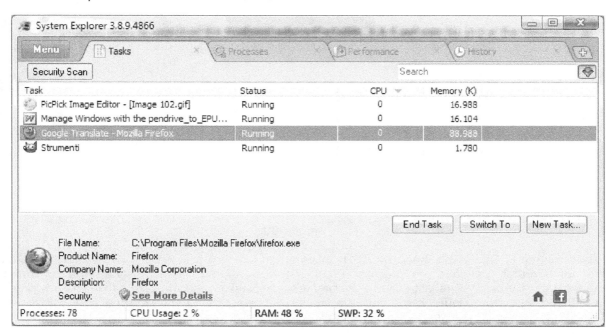

Figure 78

The initial screen shows the actives processes, their state and their consumption of CPU and memory
The program is very complete and analyzes the applications, processes, provides several graphs on system performance and allows you to check (with the active internet connection) if a process is suspect. We will analyze only a few components that relate to the processes and their occupation of the operating system resources. With your mouse, select the "**Processes**" tab in the figure above (Figure.78) and will see a screen like the following:

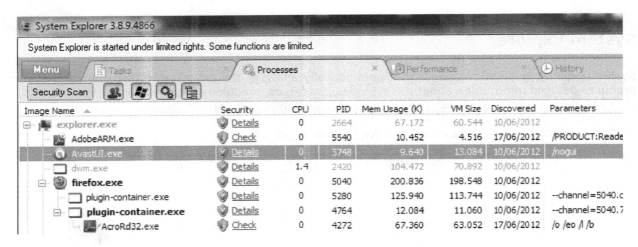

Figure 79

On the left side, under the **"Image name"** column, there are all active processes in your computer, while under the **"Security"** column there are names like **Check** or **Details**. If, with the mouse, we click on **Details** or **Check** , the "System Explorer" program search on the net, the name of the "suspect" (for example avastsvc.exe) program and in a browser screen provides information about the authenticity of program and details of the manufacturer, as shown in the screenshot below:

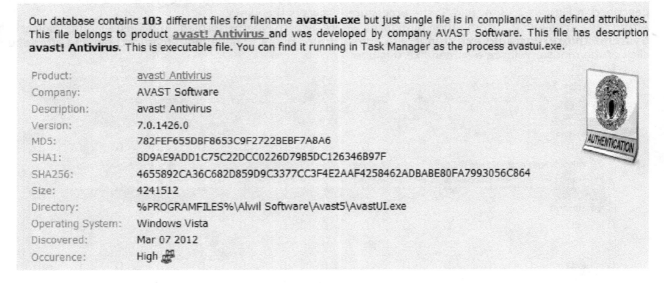

Figure 80

The third column of Figure 79, shows the CPU consumption for each process and in the fourth column there is the number that identifies the process (PID). The fifth column, instead, shows the consumption of memory for each process. The last column "Parameters" displays the parameters by which each process has been initiated. Also from Figure 79, if, with the mouse, we select the **"Performance"** tab, will see a screen that contains several graphs related to the use of the processor, the memory, the reads and writes to your hard drive:

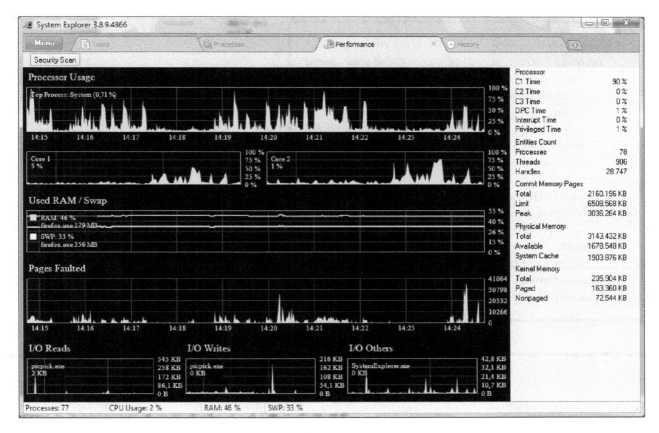

Figure 81

The last tab on the top of Figure.78 is "History"; if we select it with the mouse, we will see the following screen:

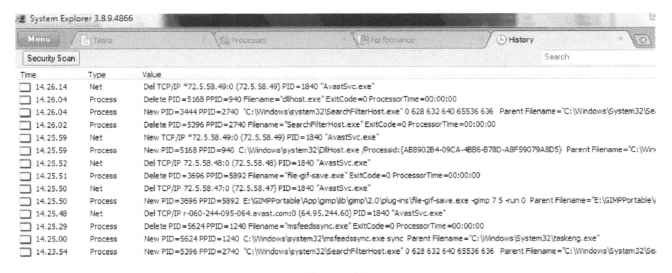

Figure 82

The screen above, lists the services and other activities that are initiated by the operating system every second. If the Figure.82, we place the mouse over any tab, then we press the right button and finally, we choose new window or simply press the + symbol after the "History" tab, will be displayed the menu like to Figure.83 when choosing an option from the menu on the left, you see a screen with details on the right of the screen:

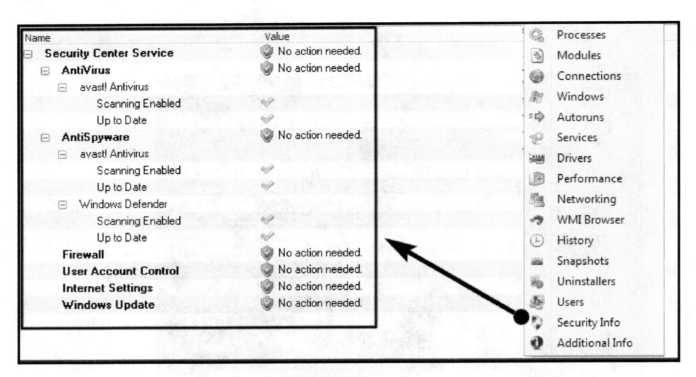

Figure 83

Uilities

Advanced Console

The utility is an enhancement of Windows console where you can keep open multiple DOS sessions. This function is interesting because sometimes when managing the operating system we run multiple DOS commands and then compare the results. The utility lets you change the background, fonts and more for every console.

It can be installed on the following operating systems: Windows 2000/XP/Vista/7.

You can download it from the following site: *http://portableapps.com/apps/utilities/console_portable*

Figure 84

We proceed, then, to download the **ConsolePortable_2.00_b148_English.paf.exe** file and at the installation as described in Figures 2, 3, 4, and 5: the procedure is always the same.

After the installation, from the directory where we have performed the installation, select the **ConsolePortable.exe** file and after double click of the mouse, will see a screen like this one:

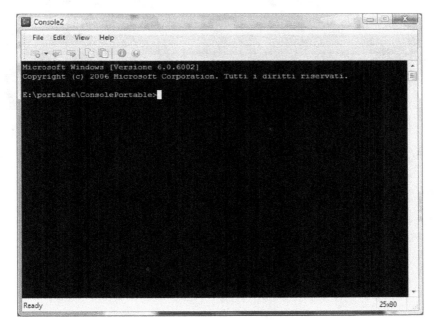

Figure 85

To create another console screen (Figure.85), with the mouse, select **"File"**, **"New Tab"**, click on **"Console2"** and the screen like this one will be displayed:

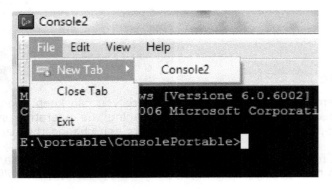

Figure 86

Figure 87

Now there are two consoles screens with the same name "**Console2**"; to change the name of a console, position the mouse anywhere on the console screen and press the right mouse button, then select "Edit", "Rename Tab" and type the new console name. You can customize each console as you want, always positioning the mouse in it, pressing the right mouse button, selecting "Edit" and then "Settings". You will see a menu where you can perform different customizations, like this one:

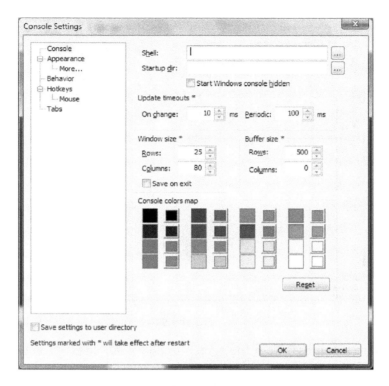

Figure 88

7-Zip

7-Zip is a utility that archives files according to the following compression types: 7z, ZIP, GZIP, BZIP2, TAR, RAR.
It can be installed on the following operating systems: Windows 2000/XP/Vista/7.
You can download it from the following site: *http://portableapps.com/apps/utilities/7-zip_portable*

Figure 89

We proceed, then, to download the **7-ZipPortable_9.20_Rev_2.paf.exe** file and at the installation as described in Figures 2, 3, 4, and 5: the procedure is always the same.
After the installation, from the directory where we have performed the installation, select the **7-ZipPortable.exe** file and after double click of the mouse, will see a screen like this one:

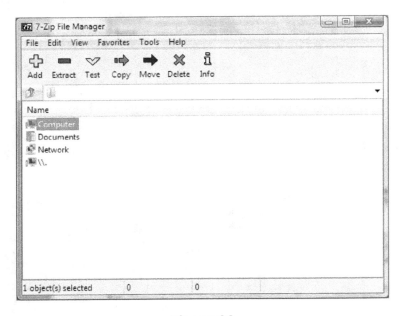

Figure 90

To choice the directory to compress, from the screen in figure 90, select "computer" icon then C drive and finally the directory (Garmin in our case):

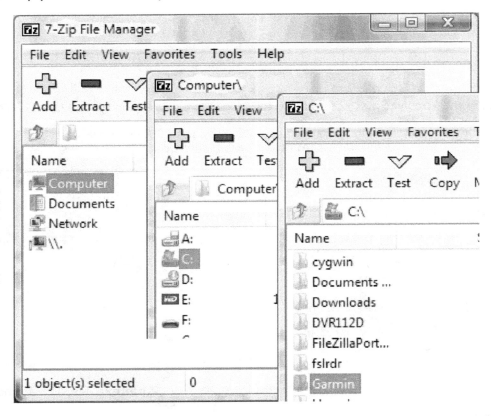

Figure 91

To compress a file or directory, select the desired object, for example, the **Garmin** directory (Figure.91), press the right mouse button, select the "**7-Zip**", then the option "**Add to archive**" as shown in the figure below:

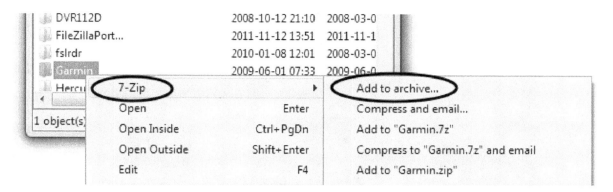

Figure 92

In the following screen, we can change the file name (if desired), and the compression type as shown by rectangles, highlighted in black colour. Press the OK button and you save a file in 7z, zip or tar in archive format.

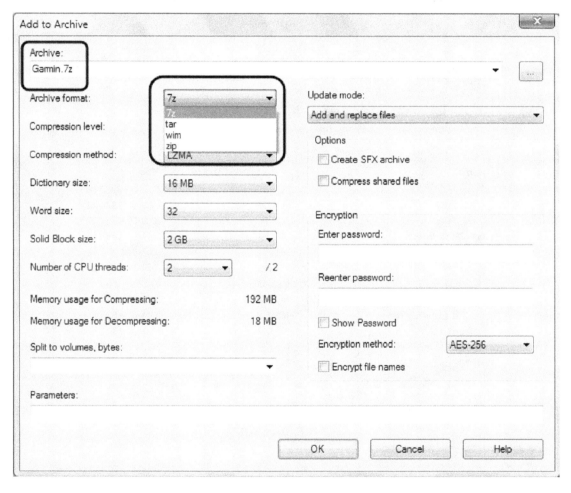

Figure 93

In this case, the compacted file will be called **Garmin.7z** because we have chosen the 7z compression. If we had chosen tar, as the archive type, the name would have been **Garmin.tar** and so on for other types of archive format.

To unzip the file, use 7-zip file manager Figure.91 and having found it, select it with the mouse and then perform a double click; will be displayed the original directory as shown in the following pictures:

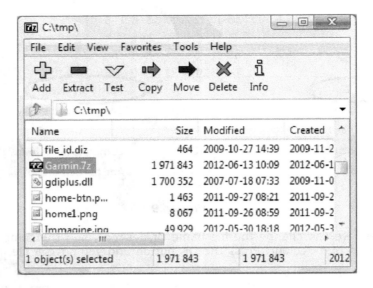

Figure 94

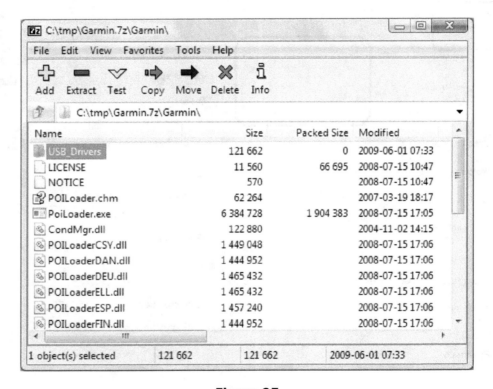

Figure 95

How to create our suite of portable software

It is possible to create our suite of portable software with a few mouse's clicks.
The program can be installed on the following operating systems: Windows 2000/XP/Vista/7 and Wine under Linux/UNIX/BSD/Mac OS X
You can download it from the following site: *http://portableapps.com/suite*

Figure 96

We proceed, then, to download the **PortableApps.com_Platform_Setup_10.0.1.exe** file and at the installation as described in Figures 2, 3, 4, and 5: the procedure is always the same.
After the installation, from the directory where we have performed the installation, select the **Start.exe** file and after double click of the mouse, will see a screen like this one:

Figure 97

To add a new application, select the menu item "**Apps**", on the right side of the screen, then "**Install a New App**", will see a screen like the following:

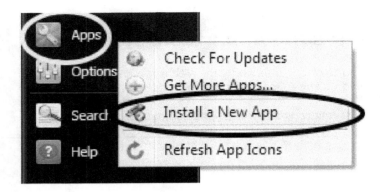

Figure 98

You will see a window where you select the application (they must have the extension. **Paf.exe**) then press the button "**Open**" and then "**Run**".

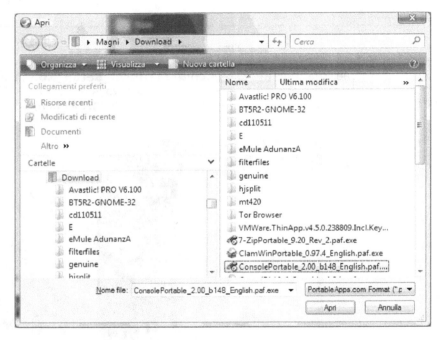

Figure 99

When finished, your first application (for instance console portable) is installed and will appear in the menu as shown below:

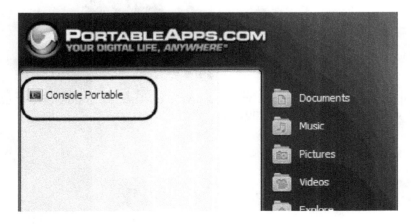

Figure 100

To install other applications; perform the same operations; choosing different files **paf.exe**. A very useful thing is the update of installed applications: from the main menu; select "**Apps**" and then "**Check for Update**". the following screens will be displayed:

Figure 101

Figure 102

If there are no updates, you will see a message to confirming it:

Figure 103

To remove the application; select it with the mouse and from the next menu, select the item "**Uninstall**".

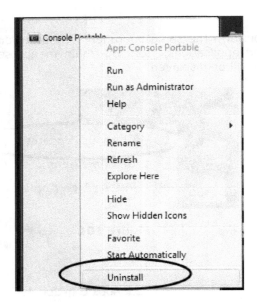

Figure 104

The following screen will appear:

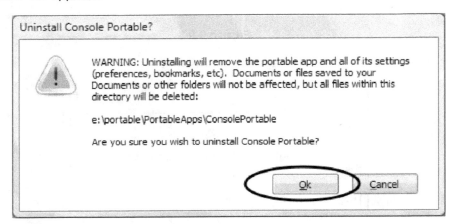

Figure 105

Pressing "**OK**" button, the application will be removed from the menu as shown in the following screen:

Figure 106

The product has many other options that I leave the reader to explore.

Suite portable ready to use

On the net we can found suite of free portable programs containing hundreds of useful applications. They are composed of a Start menu that makes it immediately available hundreds of programs. The programs are all there: the ones to listen to music, watch videos and movies; to burn cd / dvd; surf the internet; office environment; to see the images; to make the diagnostic system; to perform password recovery, to do photo editing; to synchronize an iPod; to read pdf files; read e-mails, chat on Messenger or Facebook and many other utilities.

An example of a suite of programs is **WinPenPack** that is an open source application environment for Windows; modified to run from a USB pen drive or any external media storage; without having to be installed.

Another interesting suite is **NirLauncher,** developed by NirSoft that concentrates in one place a complete set of utilities and tools to analyze and solve different problems in different areas such as Password; Networking; Audio / Video, System; Web. The suite can be used by the pen drive (USB key); and requires no installation.

Another important suite of applications is **Portable Apps** that also contains a number of programs; often made portable by the developers of package.

LiberKey proposes; instead, three types of packages: a **Small** or **Basic**; with the essential tools; an average, **Standard**; and a complete **Ultimate** with all programs.

Now we will see for example how to proceed with the installation of the last one; the others are similar.

On site *http://www.liberkey.com/en/download.html* we can choose the installation type: Basic; Standard and Ultimate.

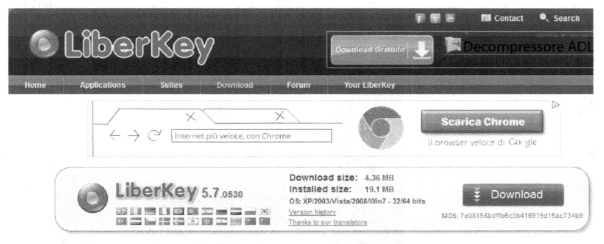

LiberKey includes direct download of **Basic, Standard** and **Ultimate** suites

Figure 107

Move the mouse over one of three types (Basic; Standard; Ultimate) and after selecting it; you see the list of applications; as shown in the figure below:

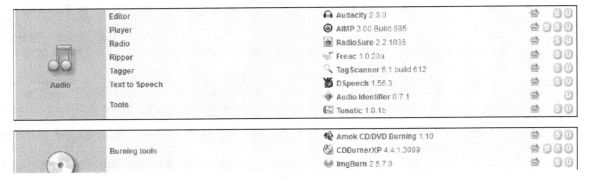

Figure 108

To download the suite; press the "**Download**" button (Figure.108); and at the end of process, the **LiberKey_5.7.0530.exe** file will be downloaded in your USB pen drive. After selecting it with the mouse and double click, will start the installation process, at the end of installation will see the following screens:

Figure 109

After holding the "**Download the list of available suites**" big button on the right side of the figure.109, we will see a screen where you can choose the installation type: Basic; Standard or Ultimate (as shown on the left side of figure.110) and the package you wish to install.

Figure 110

I recommend installing them all, pressing the button at the bottom of the screen "**Install all the applications** ..." as shown at the bottom of figure 110. After pressing this button, the following screen will appear:

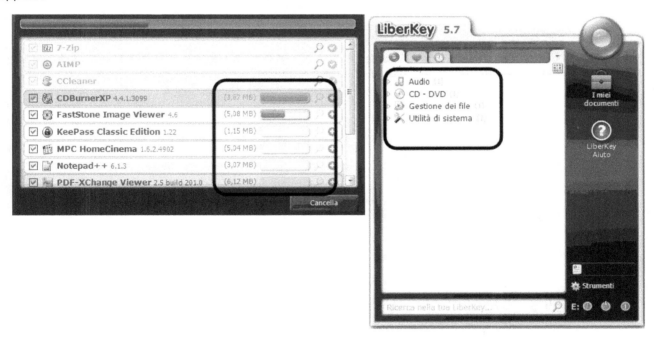

Figure 111

The installation process continues by highlighting the right side of the screen the status of the download (Figure.111 on the left, see black box); at the same time will be updated the application menu (Figure.111 on the right, see the black box).
When finished you will see a screen like the following:

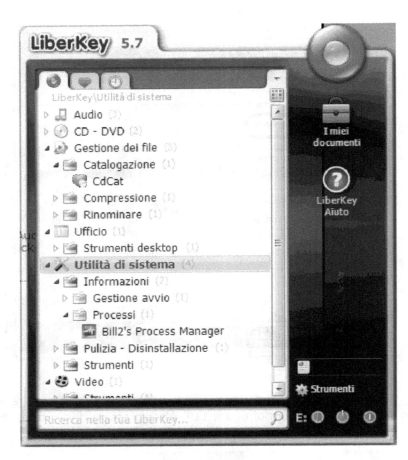

Figure 112

Selecting one of the menu items (for example, Audio, CD-DVD; File Management, etc) will be shown the list of programs available where, with the double click of the mouse, we can start the one that interests us.

How to create a portable program

Universal Extractor is a free program used to transform a program into a "portable program".
It can be installed on the following operating systems: Windows 2000/XP/Vista
We download it from the following site *http://www.legroom.net/software/uniextract* , selecting; in the download section; the portable version: **UniExtract Binary Archive** and unzip to a directory in your USB pen drive.
After running it; you will see a screen like the following:

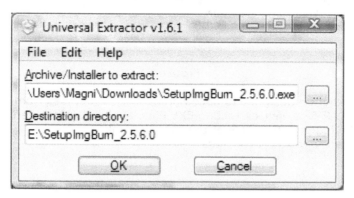

Figure 113

In the first box (**Archive / Installer to extract**); select the installation file (in our case SetupImgBurn_2.5.6.0.exe) while in the second (**Destination directory**); the destination directory where the program will be made. Press the "**OK**" button and after a few moments, all program files; will be created in the destination directory like to the image below:

Nome	Ultima modifica
$INSTDIR	13/06/2012 15.50
$PLUGINSDIR	13/06/2012 15.50
$TEMP	13/06/2012 15.50
file0021.bin	13/06/2012 15.50
file0022.bin	13/06/2012 15.50
script.bin	13/06/2012 15.50

Figure 114

The file that will start the "portable program", is the one with **exe** extension. Sometimes it happens that this file is inside other subfolders, created by Universal Extractor during the process, not visible in the initial screen of the parent folder (figure.114). We check all the folders to find the **exe** file. In our case it is in the **$INSTDIR** folder and to run it, simply double-click of the mouse after selecting it:

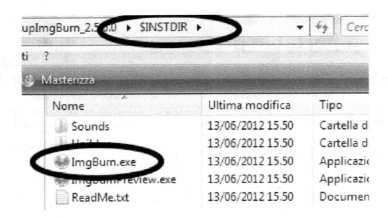

Figure 115

Universal Extractor is a program designed to decompress and extract files from any type of archive or installer, such as ZIP or RAR files, self-extracting EXE files, application installers, etc. The full list of supported formats can be found in the table at the following link
http://legroom.net/software/uniextract#formats

Conclusion

Now, we have a set of tools to monitor and manage the operating system and all its components. We will use the antivirus to protect our computers and other tools to analyze and monitor all system components: disks, memory, and processes. I think that the suites proposed; is the minimum required that everyone should have in the USB pen drive, to better manage their computer. The applications that I have proposed seem to me the most interesting and complete than we can found on the net. For each portable program, I have analyzed the single feature that interested us at that time; really all the proposed portables programs have many other functions that I leave the reader explore and investigate. On the net we can found many portable programs related to the Internet, the development; the music and video, the Office environment, the safety and other utilities. If we go to the following link *http://portableapps.com/* and press the "**get apps**" button (located at the top left of the screen) will be displayed an applications' menu where individual programs and a brief explanation of their use are listed.